Dancing Embers

DANCING EMBERS

Sándor Kányádi

translated from the Hungarian by Paul Sohar

TWISTED SPOON PRESS • PRAGUE • 2002

ISBN 80-86264-04-1

Contents

The publisher Kurt Wolff wrote that one of the essential tools of his profession is familiarity with world literature, not just that of his own country. This cannot be disputed. It must be so, too, for the reader. Yet it is a grievous fact that there are essential poets and novelists whom we readers find almost by accident. So often it falls to the small presses and the little magazines to bring us their work; particularly in translation. That privilege was mine (among others) as editor and publisher of a small magazine, *Archipelago* (www.archipelago.org), when several years ago I was offered a sheaf of poems of Sándor Kányádi translated by Paul Sohar. I was then (as Wolff no doubt would not have been) unfamiliar with the parlous situation of Transylvanian Hungarians and the poet Kányádi, whose very mother tongue had for decades been under assault. Among the poems, his "All Souls' Day in Vienna" remained in my ear. It was as if composed in a voice half-heard, half-overheard; yet something great moved through it. I wished to, I would publish it. Yet mine was the most difficult of a reader's task, to consider the translation as a poem in itself. Although its historical references and cultural allusions were essential to its meaning, it should speak beyond them to a shared quality, some aspect of spirit, in order to *come across* in this language as vital.

As a reader, then, I sought a common standpoint from where to begin. This was a poem of deep, grinding sorrow, a religious poem, as I read it, which (like much of Kányádi's poetry, it seems) employed the subversive irony of art in magnificent, hopeless defense against a God — or an earthly ruler — by whom no absolution is given. In that sense, it was a quarrel with an absent god. And so, perhaps caustically, the poem begins in a church, the poet leaning against a pillar listening to the music. My standpoint, then, was that white Augustinerkirche in Vienna, once the capital of the Hapsburgs (where I too had attended the Sunday concert-mass and

11

heard Mozart played).

In the poem, it is All Souls' Day, the day of atonement and sorrow for the dead. Mozart's Requiem is being sung. The poet, a man of earthly tastes, is far from home. In his lonely eye is another scene of mourning. A coffin bobs on weak shoulders in a heavy rain and slips away into the mud, and the mud-slurry sweeps it down the great Danube to the sea . . . The miserable burial of Mozart shamed the court and society he had served. The braided wreath — funeral; laurel — remains his only honor.

The artist's life is precarious and full of chagrin. His humiliation is complete, even as the glory of his music rises to the heavens: but (asks the poet, suddenly furious): *Is god pleased with praises sung by / men who've had their balls cut off . . . ?* While even *the inhabitants of the most godforsaken / les plus lointaines civilizations . . . / would perk up their ears only on hearing / mozart's music . . .*

In his mind's eye the poet sees and mourns the "godforsaken" of his own country, who are standing

> *With gaggling geese / quacking ducks / lice-ridden chickens / scab-covered piglets / from a shared little yard / filthy little brats / conceived in boozy haze / in a mob are gaping / at the sky streaked by planes / faster than the speed of sound*

They are country people — the poet mocks their mockers — awed yet left behind by the modern world.

The poet is carried back in time, to 1944 and the awful bombing of Nagyvárad. There, too, were people just trying to live, while from the sky those streaking airplanes bombed them. The poet cries out: Is this atonement for ancient sins, for which we must pay and pay, and keep on paying? Where God should have been (I imagined) are the planes with bombs. Fire rains from the sky upon the children, and *who fears hell for this— the one / who lost or the one who won?*

Dies irae dies illa.

The poet begins to comprehend the awful price that he, too, has to pay for looking too hard, even for writing a sentence, which *starts to scratch / hinting at a red alarm.*

What are the ancient sins that must be pardoned?* This poem has been compared (Paul Sohar tells us) to Eliot's "The Waste Land," with reason. And as Eliot had evoked pagan and Christian motifs in the cascading voices of his poem, so — I considered — had Kányádi not (perhaps) similarly counterpoised Lutheran motifs against the oppressiveness of the symbolic white church of the Augustines? Let me consider Luther and the nature of sorrow. In his great quarrel with the Church, himself still an Augustinian monk, Luther argued that the primitive notion of Christian sorrow — that the sinner repents of having offended God because of his pure love of Him — had been corrupted by the ecclesiastical sale of indulgences. So, institutionally, a man's sorrow was turned into a sort of barter or commerce, merely a formal act; and the action of his heart in relation to God was displaced. Lutheranism is not my faith, yet I learn it is Kányádi's. I read his poem, then, as the argument of a man shaken to the core of his heart by sorrow in this world, yet who is armed with a wit sharpened by sardonic near-despair into an inverted language of belief. *[T]he most godforsaken . . . / would perk up their ears only on hearing / mozart's music,* as if music — the perfect art — were the only solace possible.

Historically, Luther's theses against the commerce of indulgences turned on the nature of sorrow before God; but his enemy the papal nuncio, also an Augustinian, "had not to deal with the opposition of a recalcitrant monk but with the awakening of a nation." Is not Kányádi, also, calling upon his braided nation to

---

* In response to an earlier draft, Paul Sohar wrote: "'All Souls' Day' is mostly about Hungary's (unavoidable) participation in WWII on the wrong side. Romania was in the same situation, but they were able to switch sides when the Russians were at their border. The present situation (1960-1970) is seen as a consequence of that disastrous war, punishment for the evils of the war, regardless of who committed them. (For example, the bombing of Nagyvarad[sic] . . . was during the war, most likely by Americans.)" Sohar's extended comments about this complex poem have been very helpful to me.

maintain their communal strength in the face of — human; government-caused — terror? The ancient Székelers, it is written, were free men, all being equal in the saddle, all having equal voice before their ruler. Perhaps it was somewhat as, in a fine, plain, moving verse, the poet remembers life on the family farm.

> *Indeed our farm was no big deal / not even god could make us kneel / by hook or crook / we managed fine / complaining was not our line / from custom though we used to pray / to keep the old reaper away*

Here, one reads, is one of the oldest themes of Hungarian poetry: "God, family life, homestead." Do these lines not evoke the "splendid" Székeler ballads and folk-songs, "striking examples of an animated imagination endowed with a sense of the concrete"? "Here I stand; I can do no otherwise. God help me. Amen!" Luther cried: as the poet cries; but with whom does the poet stand? Again he counterpoises belief against belief. He stands as if with the meanest peasants (as Luther their betrayer would not). He stands with his own powerless people, for their life on their earth.

Side by side I poised the Latin, an English translation of the Requiem, and Paul Sohar's translation of "All Souls' Day in Vienna," as the poem invited one to do. Kányádi calls upon the resources of Hungarian poetry (as Eliot did his own tradition) with references to history, the ballad, the vernacular tongue, the lyric, the visionary poem, love of homeland, the survival of his Transylvanian people, God and Jesus; calling as intercessors the good king Matthias Corvinus and Lajos Kossuth, the great leader of the common people. I could only propose correspondences. I could not (quite) hear the tone or the subtleties of inflection, but infer them, from the translation. Was the movement of the Requiem that of the poem? I thought it was, or was similar to it, but darkly, for the poem ends not with the prayer *Let perpetual light shine upon them*, but a dry, Eliotian aside: Things could be worse; they might be; but we still have a bit of faith, a little something to believe in — unless they take that away, too. The poet is full of bitter mockery, and self-mockery, but also (at moments) solaced by art. In one of his strongest, most beautiful passages, Kányádi wryly notes the necessity of myth in a life — faith in God; faith in the plain things of daily life (*what else we need / something to eat*) — even as he welcomes the healing joy of the music, while hearing, loving, the milk murmurs, the lowing cows.

> *the myth and mass just keep on purling / the soprano leaps from trill to trill / dispensing such unearthly calm / that only eden could instill // the cornmeal's halo steams / the hungry children's dreams // milk murmurs of / milk whirring / milk gurgling / so sweetly / so velvety // what else we need / something to eat / what else we need / to make the blissful / evening complete . . . // let me have the strength to stay here / and feel my endless blessings fizz / where the night is painted black / by murderous futilities // but neither science nor an eye / can see that a small firefly / transports me to a distant nest / so death and I can say good-bye*

In this moment — his "Recordare," perhaps — the poet identifies himself with, becomes, one of the godforsaken; one of the people of the farmstead, even as he leans against the pillar in the Augustinian church. "Here I stand; I can do no other." Here, in this place, among the homely life of the Hungarian people. Surely this passage, built upon earlier verses of farm and home, is the emotional heart of the poem. I cannot not help but think of (the secular) Brahms before Eliot, and of the poem as A Transylvanian Requiem.

Katherine McNamara
January 2002

Note: I have quoted lines from Kányádi in italics. Remarks about Luther and Hungarian history, including quotations, are drawn from various articles in the *Encyclopaedia Britannica*, Eleventh Edition. "God, family life, homestead" and "splendid" Székeler ballads and folk-songs, "striking examples of an animated imagination endowed with a sense of the concrete" is from "Hungarian Poetry," *The Princeton Encyclopedia of Poetry and Poetics*, Enlarged Edition (1967, 1974).

That was the answer a schoolchild in a village gave on one of my reading tours of the countryside. What is a poem? was the question, his own, and he had addressed it to me, obviously prompted by the teacher. Caught off-guard I tossed the question back to him the way the frightened soldier in old war stories would return the still unexploded hand grenade.

"Well, what do you think a poem is?"

"A poem is something . . ." he was clinging to my gaze for encouragement, "you have to tell."

Laughter rippled through the classroom . . . Only the two of us stood there in awe.

He, mostly out of relief at having rid himself of that boomerang, but also in gratitude for my not joining in the general laughter.

I, from the realization that this schoolchild had found a simple way to formulate the truism I had long entertained but was unable to put into plain words.

A poem is something you have to tell.

As if I had been brushed by a breeze stirred up at the beginning of time.

As if Homer, startled from his slumber, had opened his blind yet light-filled eyes at me.

As if poems exiled into books since Gutenberg had risen and hurried back home, to stand up at the podium or on the TV screen, to sing marching on tape or dancing around on a turntable.

As if Sándor Petőfi, our national poet, had sat down among us.

A poem is something you have to tell.

Vertical Horses
1963-1968

SMOKE

Smoke has been the sign of human settlement
ever since Prometheus' defiant act,
ever since people settled down to roasting,
torching, scorching and cremating, ever since
human history began its smoldering.

The pale blue smoke of campfires and
the black smoke of plunder, burning stakes,
and crematoria; they both have stained the sun
and its starry vault in this accustomed homey hue.

Puffing on a cigarette I'm sitting high up on a hill,
watching limpid supper smoke weave its way
from the valley across the reclining sunrays;
but it's the sickening fume of burning brains
that tickles my memory for taste and smell.

Could they be burning books somewhere?

On that evening the sky was like a deserted town
with the lights left on by the panic-stricken
population in their headlong escape. And yet,
portents and ominous signs were nowhere in sight,
only at dawn did the advance units start to appear
slowly, with caution: just a few squadrons of mist.
Then the armies marched in, starting the invasion
from the north, east and west — southward.
The arc-lights of the Milky Way were snuffed out one by one,
the Dippers fell off the wall along with the candles. Then,
total darkness. The occupation of the sky by the clouds was
complete and a day of plunder was declared. Right away
the locked formations of the well-disciplined troops were broken,
and the crazed sacking began; the conquerors smashed and crashed,
ripped out the plumbing, broke the windows and tossed out
the still flaming candelabras. They were driven by the
impotent fury of having been cheated: they found no one at home,
                                        no one
in hiding, no one resisting, no woman or child, not even a baby
                                        to splatter
against the wall, no one. They slashed open the pillows,
                                        the mattresses,
and after a while, since there was nothing else to do, they
                                        declared peace.

And now peace prevails. It's snowing.

SPRING BALLAD

Snaketime, betrayal-scented dawn!
Paralyzed stands the apricot tree
looking around her as if trapped,
on her frost-veiled rosy cheeks the plea
stiffens into a lifeless, frozen fact.

With feigned holiness and grace
a flabby-cassocked sun
sprinkles its absolving rays: to your virgin army,
oh Lord, add another one.

— Ophelia, my Ophelia! — From my soul I wrench
the name as grieving gardens
start to fill with medieval stench.

Like a star the girl was bathing,
swimming through the arms of light
and shadows to scale the other shore,
a flesh-and-blood water sprite.
Took a dip and "Let's have the next!"
Late into the night that's how
it went until her father, brother
and intended found her under plow:
they pummeled and kicked her where they could,
old gypsy fortunetellers hexed
her writhing hips, her clenched bare teeth,
her wet face pressed in sand, and next
they left her lying on the brink
of death, but by the morning she
could wink again at soldiers. Surely
she deserved the harmony
of songs and poems to woo
her — more than so many other sluts
who have had madrigals and
sonnets dedicated to their butts —
but the devoted rookie troops
and the toilers from the mines
were not tutored in the art
of music and poetic lines.

A SONNET TO THE GYPSY GIRL

On the lawn, you dusky nymph,
my cape will let us lie at ease,
you won't catch a nasty cold
and the grass won't stain my knees.

Let the darkness of your locks and
full-moon eyes enthrall me blind,
my hands will pump a fire dance with
the bellows of your bare behind.

A pyramid, you string of pearls,
I'll build for you of all the girls;
my cape is wetter than the lawn,

come you pharaoh's child and let
the devla take your scarf, my debt
I'll settle like a lord at dawn.

Devla: Romani for devil.

PONDERING STANDS THE MAN

Dawn is drizzling hot pigeon blood
instead of dew;
light is squinting on the hillside,
a quiver runs through the locust tree.

A barefoot boy is trudging along
in the shivering goose bumps
of the trail's dust,
his bleeding heels sow freckles
on the thirst-bent grass.

It's still the same old trail,
and the grass leaning into it
still has the same bloody rust spots;
Blood-of-Christ grass — as some say.

Pondering stands the man,
his eyes plowing the trail
he asks in a low mutter:
was it my blood or could it
have come from Heaven?

AT THE END

And then the ocean floods the world.
I can still hear my dear mother call me
by my name from the murk of a past dusk,
while the blind butterfly from the oil lamp in her hand
flies into the window of our cottage.
And then the ocean floods the world,
the Sun and the Moon rocking wondrous-
shaped ships in their wake.
Only an orphan pear tree still waves to me
from this world turned shoreless.

ONE SINGLE REED

The sedge was burned down recently,
now black cinder, soot and slow
subsiding, orphaned shadows are
mourning themselves on the snow.

There's no reed to zing against another,
the vale can whisper not a sound,
a single stalk is left there howling
stranded in the icy pond.

A skeleton of its former self,
this singly standing ragged reed
alone can be heard

screeching, scratching bloody
wings against the gleaming ice;
a flightless, wounded bird.

Sticks once chased him from house to house,
and then clear out of town.
Now between two towns he
scampers up and down.

Once he was a bold one,
apt to snap back at the stick.
Take a look at him now:
there's no sight more sad and sick.

Even a bird can spook him,
his sinews are a steady shake,
his teeth persist there in the mouth
all for chatter's sake.

On his tongue the warts seek water,
without it he is sure to waste.
Around his jaws the spit and tears
congeal into a slimy paste.

He weeps. He'd like to howl but
then he might be overheard —
Trying to save his hide for nothing
while his legs can still be stirred.

Trying to save his hide for nothing.
His hide is but an empty sack —
Merciful hunter,
what's holding you back?

We retreated into the cellar,
behind vats and mounds of carrots;
we had to squash and squeeze against each other:
farthest behind and almost underneath
the nubile girls disguised as old hags
with black kerchiefs and soot smeared on their cheeks.
Outside there was marching, wagons and guns and
tanks were rumbling: the front line was
either retreating or advancing. A warmth
started to radiate within me,
the same kind I used to feel
on spring nights on the hard
boarding school bed:
outside the armies were beginning
to rumble to the beat of the
re-opened power plant;
it was as if another body had been
hooked into my blood circulation: a pair
of tightly squeezed thighs, a pair of
panting breasts were advancing closer and closer.
The girls were tittering, the wilted lads were
shushing. "The others are doing the same thing,
you silly ass," whispered a hand,
not under my clothes but my skin.
"A grown lad you are, lucky thing
for you I'm not on the draft board,"
said a young war widow laughing
as she straightened out her skirt
with an experienced hand when
the door was opened, giving an all
clear signal; and she followed behind

the soot-smudged girls as they marched out
in single file with eyes downcast
up the cellar steps.
Her two bent knees kept the cellar bright
with their beauty
for some time.
And as to the war?
I declared victory.

Knobby fingers,
slowly bending
measured hooks,
deaf-and-mute
to freeze or fire,
ember-pinching fingertips.

The ember's dancing;
a firebrand selected from live embers for
a hoary death inside a pipe.

It's dancing in a dirt-encrusted hand,
amidst the five throbbing hearts of five fingertips,
the ember's dancing.

It's dancing in the exalted hand
of Prometheus,
on the callused palms
of hobnobbing old peasants as well as
Indian chiefs lighting up their calumets, and
amidst the five shivering hearts of Petőfi's five fingertips
in his garret's chill.

From fire to death.

The loneliness of fire glowing
in a asphalt-crusted concrete waste,
in a rough-hewn valley of the Moon,
held by an asbestos hand.

A fish tossed ashore
by a sea of fire.

The war's been dragging on for millennia.
Sometimes there is a break, a breather,
to gather new strength, to beget posterity
who will carry on the struggle
so that those coming in the footsteps of the Blind Bard
can properly memorialize everything;
at times like these the victorious Agamemnon, too,
used to come home to visit with his family.
When I knew him he had just returned
from a POW camp along with Odysseus,
but in the meantime his wife had taken up with a horse trader
who, however, didn't kill the old soldier and so
the children didn't have a murder to avenge.
He drowned his sorrows in drink, went on the skids.
At the end, for a shot of brandy, he would tell of
his glorious exploits on the battlefield:
from Troy to the distant Don River.
He kept swearing that one day he would kill Clytemnestra
along with that cowardly crook who here, in his home,
while he, out there . . . They laughed at him, but then
gave him the bum's rush when they got tired of him.
He made his home in a sand pit, that was
where he froze to death in that winter described
in the papers as:
"The worst in recent memory . . ."
Electra and Orestes were engaged elsewhere and unable
to attend the funeral paid for by public donations,
but they were there in spirit: "It was all for the best.
May God forgive his sins. It's a big load
off our minds."

THE MUTE

At times I still hear infants'
marrow-piercing howl.
Europe speaks in many chords.
Not only the muses of Helicon but
the babies thrown off Mount Taygetus
deafened the gods of fate.

The millennia of howling,
the plucking of harps and zithers,
the beating of drums,
the roar of bells and engines,
the shelling and the bombing,
have blasted out an atmospheric
pressure cave,
rendering us hard of hearing.
Taygetus has taken root in us.
Our shoelaces can undo themselves.

All it takes is one hard look, the wave of a hand,
and we fall in line, dumb and numb,
some with head held high, some deeply bent,
but we all obey the call.

There was a deaf-mute living next door,
a real hard-working beast of burden,
they'd kept his nose to the grinding stone
till he turned into one.

When the Spartan Home Security came to pick
him up though, he earned a place in history:
he grabbed a pitchfork and started

to kick, bite and claw
like he used to as an infant,
and he howled too, but as an adult.

COPY

Everything's been written,
even that which had been written.
Slowly life itself will
feel like an afterthought.
The typewriter writes by itself,
knocking off nothing but
second and third copies.
Strontium and carbon paper.
Why is it that sensitive instruments
can only detect the danger of strontium?
I just heard on the radio:
five-thousand-year-old clay tablets
were discovered somewhere,
probably the copies of well-known clay tablets
inscribed a thousand years earlier.

VERTICAL HORSES

to the sculptor Viktor Roman

When a horse crumples to his rump
he lets his forelegs hang limp like
a begging dog and the hooves
split into finger-like fragments
one long neigh stretches the neck
upwards by the slender head
till they both rise in one taut vertical line
the length of a horse

the shock of the eye sockets' emptiness
balloons the eyeballs out
and the sky thickens into a cataract
the tongue slips down into the throat
the testicles explode
under the animal's crushing weight

And yet the pain of horses sitting upright
redoubles when it starts to torture the ten
fingertips objectively sculpting
a voiceless statue
out of horror

AND YET

The evening sky provokes
no poetic comment from me.
We're getting closer to the ground.
The soul is sated with metaphors;
we have better tools at our disposal
than similes for illustration;
exaltation is gathering dust
in the attic or the cellar,
bundled together with defunct currency;
words pool into lakes,
pathos floats on them in oil slicks,
who cares how we relate to our times:
to live is the point.
And yet:
like a ship the moon floats in the sky's ocean.
Just the way it did in the evening
of the space-probe landing.
How did that probe land?
Like a seagull on a ship.

FALL

Serves no good for the steeples
to keep stabbing at the sky,
the peals of the church bells
ooze out like the fog.
Somewhere an old granny
pokes at the loam
with a stick,
one glance of hers encloses
the Universe
in the abandoned
barnyard.

NUMBED NIGHTMARE

The same old dream: I am the child
playing on the tracks again,
I stand there numb and let the world
hit me like I'd let the train.

A squirming scream inside me
gives my lips a silent twitch:
I can see my head roll off
the tracks and down into a ditch.

OBJECTS

Objects slowly take on our
features, habits and play our parts.
The table and the bed identify
with us becoming our guards.

The spoon, the glass, the fork, the cup,
all are body parts we share.
One's body slowly tires into
a mere fixture for one's chair.

Pictures, records, books and statues,
carefully preserved bouquets
form an alliance with the wall and
soon the room inside us stays.

They usurp our longings and then
they get bored with us, our whine,
and playing off our sinews against us
they lay us on a board of pine.

HORSES

Humanity and storms,
even time itself,
used to ride on horseback.

It is from the backs of
galloping horses that
supersonic planes take off:

at the edge of the runway
the leaves of grass flutter like
the mane of a leaping horse.

FROM TREE TO TREE

From tree to tree now dusk is creeping
from tree to tree a kid is stealing
My God, he'll never make it
back on foot
unless the sun forgets to set over the clearing
or if I could only hear the horse's bell

He freezes now and then, ready to sprint,
like a squirrel his teeny heart would sneak off and hide
among the anxious poplar leaves
but where are they now
the faithless poplars are stranded in a clearing
no bigger than your palm or a penny
Galloping home I'll grab
the horse's mane
but now just a little farther
to that fat beech tree, the fifth from here

Rather be a fox, a wolf, a deer
a tree limb, a bush or loam
a bird nest
an egg
a poplar leaf
or a coo-coo call
anything but a little kid
tracking down stray horses

I'll pass just two more trees or four
I can hear it, I cannot, and yet I can
If I make it to that ash tree
I'll be a warrior, a ship's captain,

I'll discover America and if America
gets lost I'll find it again

On the way home I'll grab the mane
One more tree Or maybe three
I'll be a prophet and a healer
I'll be Jesus
and resurrect my mother from the dead
Just a little farther I can hear it
"Up the steeple the April's fool
climbed one day right after school
asking what the time was
Half past two
Climbed the steeple after school"

Now it's quiet, they must be standing still,
well-fed now they slumber
Let the hounds rip their bellies
or let the wolves
Should be all right to cry and sing
to become the night
or just nothing,
shouldn't take another step

Strayed too far, Where's the clearing?
I'll count only five more trees and then
"How the devil only knows
Honey on the bear cub's nose"

The bell is ringing, I still can hear it
I've strayed too far, Where's the clearing?
From here I can still find my way back
I'll drop crumbs
cross-twig marks
carve my name into the bark

The bell is ringing, I still can hear it
it's been ringing all along
already in my mother's womb

The sun will wait for me
and so will the poplars
Foxy dusk and wolfish night
keep on creeping from tree to tree
push yourself, you little lad

Nothing to hear and still you hear it
The moon is over the clearing now
But it's about to set
Your crumbs have all been gobbled up
and your cross-twig marks overgrown

Your name's a blistered hieroglyph
On a dead branch hangs the bell
the wolves have got your horse
The forest is a jungle now
Mother's milk
Moth's milk

On and on from tree to tree
"Honey on the bear cub's nose
that's where every deerfly goes"

The road has slipped out from under you
The quake of poplars has settled
on the poles of your brow
But keep it up from tree to tree
It's not a reel of film or tape
that could be put in fast reverse

Branches offer themselves
philosophers are dangling a noose
"C'est la vérité monsieur"
"Die letzte Lösung mein Herr"
"It's almost twelve o'clock
a fool plus fool makes a flock"

On and on from tree to tree
stealing yourself
stumbling reeling
Mother's milk
Moth's milk
Vinegar

Black-and-Red Verses
1965-1972

CAGED IN

Snap your jaws across my throat
don't just stand there looking wild.
He who hesitates is apt to miss the boat,
don't just wait before the beast
in me, too, might get riled.

And then what? Europe can shed
again its precious cultured tears,
and for us the same old song of
repentance we've been taught for years.

What are you waiting for? It's my blood
your eyes are so enamored of.
You'll get over any pangs
of conscience easily enough.

As the cheapest belly fodder
the human body rates.
Don't fret, it's only itself that
history regurgitates.

Don't let it spoil things that I look
upon this feast so sad and gaunt;
I was born before my time,
and that was purely my own fault.

BALLAD

The wind is whistling lead pellets
the engines are puffing
out gunpowder
blood sprays on
the swirling leaves
while a bushy reed with
a broken ankle is drooping
out of an abandoned tin
wastebasket
like a young rabbit
out of a hunter's haversack

Brueghel was hard at work all night,
that's how the picture is preserved,
the bright rays of memory could never
thaw the frost-fettered
seedling rows nor the severity
of the crow's-feet branches.
These crows will
never take off
from the ice-bearded power lines.
I glimpse the breath of bristly peasants
on a village station platform whizzing by
and clamorous children
cheering the ice in a ditch.
Then a hand — maybe
the master's — pulls down the shade
over the window.

Even the immortals knuckled under: Zeus accepted
Jupiter as his new name as long as he could keep his rank
and dignity but especially his job. After that, who can blame
the simple goatherds, the seafarers, the craftsmen,
the tradesmen who went on with business as usual, paying taxes
and offering sacrifices just like before? A few hot-headed
clerics and poets kept up the bravado at the beginning,
but then even they were bought off by the clever Romans
who managed to buy up history and get a lease on mythology.
That's how, out of Greek, Etruscan and nameless other scattered
stones, there was created the great pastiche: Rome. Jupiter *tonat*
(thunders, as we learned in Latin class) and then Aphrodite under
the new
name Venus became a star in Cinecitta, and the pretty but mute
maid of the Etruscan vase took a job smiling as a model in a
fancy department store. (She can do well there without the
command of the language.) Poseidon alone will not make
peace even though he's got a new statue in every town erected under
his new name, the purling water fountains can't seem to soothe his
wrath. On his more relaxed days he takes a stand in front of the
commanding ruins of his temple in Paestum and, leaning on his
trident,
he watches the ox herd graze among the laurels of the sacred grove
while the gaping tourists gather for an enactment of the Greek rites:
wunderbar, beautiful, merveilleuse — the shutters are clicking, the
camcorders are humming; an old war veteran is putting on a big
show of pointing out the monuments and at the end he humbly
holds out his hand, groveling with a grin: *thank you,*
danke schön, merci, grazie, grazie tante.

RAIN

after a long drought when finally
it starts to pour drumming on the roof
the ancient toiler of the land stretches out in me
                                    to anatolia
time and space crackle in my bones
my happiness reaches the splendid
equinox of love
my heart picks up the subtly
varying beat of the rain
and I feel the thirst-drunk soil
slowly relax

BLACK-AND-RED

*A descriptive poem I penned about the
traffic island located between Kolozsvár's
Telephone Center and the old Millrace
in the nineteen sixties and seventies on
Thursday and Sunday afternoons.*

On Thursdays when it's black and red
and on Sunday afternoons
— the maids have time off from their spoons —
the sidewalk curb begins to tread
in dance steps of slow
black-and-red.

A hand clenched blue into a fist.
A tune without a lyricist.
Girls in pairs, more and more,
swirls of black, red-and-black
dancing corps.

The phone center of Kolozsvár
has solid walls that cannot bar
the world from waltzing in and out
unbarred windows' silent route

Girls in pairs, more and more,
swirls of black, red-and-black
dancing corps.

A tape deck whirs on just like this,
when it dubs in fast advance.

Weep or not, the boots must prance,
stomping to the dizzy dance:

Magyar woe and Tartar game,
they stole away my heart's own flame.
Let the winner take her sack!
The corner curb now starts to tread
in dance steps of fast
black-and-red.

It's like dancing on a raft
or a roof about to skid,
reeling on a sinking isle,
on a floating coffin lid.

Neon branches overhead
a sea of light on light pools shed!
The lamp is lit with vinegar,
the lamp is lit with vi–ne–gar.

Mother, mother, dear old mom,
why did you leave me in this prom?

Flares up to croon
a wandering tune
— that maybe I alone,
the tone-deaf can hear
whose songs can only point
but lips can never clear —
flares up to croon
a wandering tune,
a candle in the draft,
snuffed out soon.

On the banks of Szamos
almonds bloom;
the corner curbstones love to tread

in dance steps of smooth
black-and-red.

Round and round
and around
on rebound
from the ground
to the sky
eye-to-eye
not aside:
girls in pairs, more and more,
swirls of black, red-and-black
dancing corps.

Where are they from, whose brain, whose hand,
wherefrom is this motion-land?

From the marts of bombed-out forts,
from far pastures coming forth,
sent up from sage
campfires next to yurts and tents and shacks
by catapulting
wrists and hips and backs?

Or from a misty golden age?
From some prehistoric foggy ink
re-created by — instinct?
Like almond eyelids' glory
in mother-womb's
hallowed laboratory?

Where are they from, whose brain, whose hand,
wherefrom is this motion-land?
What kind of hidden walkie-talkies

receive it and transmit it here
on the matching wavelengths that
the brain and blood can commandeer?

A hand clenched blue into a fist.
A tune without a lyricist.

Girls in pairs, more and more,
swirls of black, red-and-black
dancing corps.

And on and on the tape deck whirs.
You get it when you play it back:
the manger's bliss, the coffin's curse.

Black and red, in addition to the ubiquitous white, make up the color scheme
of the folk costume popular in the Kolozsvár area.

EPIGRAMS IN MEMORY OF JANUS PANNONIUS

I
an era pregnant with murderous epigrams
may dawn upon the poets living today
but only if they don't bother
to write the murderous epigrams

II
shirts and footwear were tailored out of
the flags of freedom on the tyrant's orders
in the hope that with frequent washings
their colors would completely fade away

III
you smile at me for still marching
under the flare-flags of revolution
while others jet about on business trips

hear my answer and carve it in your brain:
look in front of your own feet and be glad
that no one has examined your fingernails

Janus Pannonius was a medieval Hungarian bishop who is considered the first
great Hungarian poet, even though he wrote hymns in Latin.

I WONDER

I wonder if instead of mother's milk
if instead of my dear mother's teats
I had grown up
on the bottle or a wet nurse
to take my first steps and then
stretched out tall to be a man
I wonder if I'd still be ready
to bite for what's rightfully mine
for what's rightfully ours
I wonder

Inscription on a Bell

a bronze bell is a bell
to summon the living
to bury the dead and
in times of danger
like fire or flood
or approaching hordes
to be rung like hell

Mantra

deep in neutral waters
    without human presence
in nuclear submarines
    without human presence
electronic brains compute
    without human presence
the precise and true picture
    without human presence
of the world to come
    without human presence

Sigh

how I wish that plane with
foreign markings hovering
almost standing still
above the ice floes of the frozen ocean
somewhere between
canada and iceland
could be my home and homeland

HOW MUCH LONGER

this non-conformist fever will burn
only until it shapes up as
a cozy tenured position
with all benefits paid

and from the backseats of power
it will look like dissent when
someone tries to keep warm by
blowing on his fingers or shuffling

      out of his row
      drifting off
      toward the back

ON MY DEATHBED

by my deathbed
someone will be there
to hold back my last gasp
until he can tape it
and play it back
for editing
so that it sounds
appropriate
or else he may erase it
so as to leave behind
nothing but this gentle smile
but of course without its bitter aftertaste
and the gasp
that gentle smile
was so characteristic
someone will say
someone whose choking grip
I have felt on my throat
all my wretched life

ALL NIGHT LONG IN FRONT

all night long in front of our
apartment house a jeep sat there
with the brake lights on
maybe it had just pulled up
or was just about to
pull out from the curb again
I always air out the room
before turning in and lean out
when closing the windows
and that's exactly what I was doing
when I caught sight of
the jeep with the taillights on
what the hell I let it slip
something wrong asked my wife
nothing at all just a jeep
what kind of jeep
some kind of a jeep I said fixing
the curtain maybe you can take
a look from here I said shrinking to
the other corner of the window
from behind the curtain
if you must
for the windows across the street
don't have to see everything I said
with a little maneuver we can
find an angle
even behind the closed window
that will afford a view
of the sidewalk or a
hand's-breath portion of it
we even welcomed this
teensy little discovery

for we had been living here
on the third floor for two decades
without realizing
how easily and without detection
we could spy on the sidewalk
I wonder if it's still there she asked
a little later under the comforter
and she kept wondering
maybe I'd better take a look and
I did and it was still there I said
with the brake lights on
looking like it had just pulled up
or was about
to pull out into the street
interesting I said and went
out to the bathroom fussed
with this and that and even started
to gargle because my throat
felt a little scratchy or who
knows what the hell
it's still there my wife whispered
giving me a start as she
whispered from behind
the curtain on my return
I squeezed beside her
and we both felt ashamed of
our audible heartbeat it'll go away
when it gets bored and back in bed
I waited and waited for her

to fall asleep so that then
I could stealthily
steal up to the window
well is it still there my wife
asked and in my distress

I said I was only
inspecting the sky
it sounded like it
might be raining
is it raining she asked
no it isn't I said and
well is it still there
it was standing there
with the taillights on
looking like it had just pulled up
or was about to pull out from the curb
yes it's still standing there even
though dawn is breaking yes it's still
there even while I am
knocking off this poem for what else
could I be doing now that
falling asleep is hopeless

BY THEIR NAMES

call them all by their names
and sketch their hands curled
in fists around a glass
a fork or an ax handle and paint the life of those
fingers and the long stretches of keeping quiet
also the days of blue and gold halved by the noontime bells
and it's time to put to use some stakes
chasing out the carousing good-for-nothings
wheat fields are not for sleeping
and the afternoons not for hoot and holler
but for quiet joy before the majestic descent of twilight
the sadness of being human

OSTINATO

I was there when the poet
was pushed around like a thief

I was there when the poet
was humiliated like a thief

I was there when the poet
was convicted as a thief

I was there and I who'd never stolen
began to tremble like a thief

LEFT BEHIND AGAIN

so we're left behind again stuck in the mud
lucky thing we have these rubber boots
and plastic rain-gear for we too are blessed
by civilization with a few things and as it is we're left here
with a pocket radio and the evening TV
but we're left behind here while culture sails off
in the distance like a giant luxury liner
for it's not the daily bread-and-lard nor the
bread-and-bacon-and-jeremiad it's not that
we could afford more except that the books
turn up their noses with a start
even though they seemed friendly at first
and eager for the candy from our hands
but then the alphabet almost got up on stilts
being so embarrassed by the poor relations

its nose is up in the air so embarrassed is
the alphabet by the poor relations

the helicopter sent to our rescue is still
circling over us but it's only for show
the ropeladder already retracted

the late descendants of prometheus would
have become fire-eaters
            such creatures and their ilk
are hopping from one theory to the next like
sparrows with frozen feet on
the frosty branches of a naked walnut tree

AN EXCHANGE OF WORDS

I carried you on my back
when you lost your legs
and instead of thanking me
you decided to grow wings

you carried me on your back
when I lost my legs
and just so I wouldn't have to thank you
I decided to grow wings

FURTIVE THOUGHTS

In Preview
this silence will prove
to be a deaf and heavy
tongueless bell
that someone will

slowly lower over us

Hungarian Made Easy
get the truth
let it shine
throw your people
a sure lifeline

Because I Am Afraid

that someday someone
may turn off the spring
the creek cascading from it
may just turn it off
out of habit like a faucet
and steadily the rivers will run dry
the seas will turn into salt flats
and the sky will fly off rattling

I'VE SEEN ENOUGH

I've seen enough
anarchists with
their eyes on a pension
penny-pinching
revolutionaries
faithless priests
— a tippling bar owner
would soon go broke —
I've been schooled
by the unschooled
— their wisely wagging fingers
even now can loom
like gallows before my eyes —
they spawned mice
in the nest of my dreams
but I remain grateful
and humble
after all I get treated
for my back pain almost gratis
at world-famous
spas
and my muse was
given a job as a ticket taker
in a museum where
eventually a picture of me
might be hung
without any hassle
ex officio so to speak

SCARECROWWEATHERCOCK
(a drama in three minutes)

(Two men enter with heads held high)

— Scarecrowweathercock.
— What's that?
— Scarecrowweathercock.
— Scarecrowweathercock?
— Exactly.
— Is this a riddle?
(shakes his head)
— What's it supposed to be? What does it mean?
— Scarecrowweathercock.
(hesitantly) — A political figure?
(shakes his head)
(they both laugh)
— What then?
— A poem.
— A poem? Maybe a title for a poem.
— A poem. A poem by itself.
— Scarecrowweathercock. Do you call that a poem, sir?
— A poem. Scarecrowweathercock. A one liner.
More precisely: a one-word poem. There is such a thing, sir.
— And what else?
— Mute.
— Mute?
— Yes.
— A mute poem?
— A mute poem. But it appears only on the inside pages.
Sometimes in large numbers. Usually as a counter-poem for
one-word poems such as mentioned above.
(silence)

— Thank you for this little essay on poetry.

— Sir.

— It should serve as consolation, too. From now on,
when words are about to form blood clots inside me,
words that are not to be uttered, I'll try to fancy myself
a great poet. Thank you.

— Don't mention it, my fellow poet.

(With heads hanging, they exit)

Curtain

Now and then my childhood's
smoke-smelling
covered wagon caravan
rumbles onto the scene
to pass before my eyes
    the tale is told about a gaping child
who got snatched
from here and there
who had his
tongue ripped out
with glowing hot pincers
and turned into a mangy dog
tied by chain under the wagon so he would
never stick his tongue out at gypsies again
    and perhaps they never
did move on but are
still camping out here
even now at the edge of the village
they are the ones who
at dusk
shake out the night
from their huge soiled sacks

WORK SONG

a pair of oxen with their weight
put to work could show their worth
a pair of stubborn oxen could
pull this overloaded earth

so their weight was put to work
with all their might they went for broke
the pair of oxen put their weight
cracking creaking in the yoke

let the yoke frame shatter into
exploding constellation signs
through the fog and smoke the word
shows itself to us and shines

on the rising new horizon
where the dying wheezes greet
the hoola-hooping cracks of whips
footprints left by naked feet

SUMERIAN SONNET

the sumerian priest appears
and takes possession of the city
I gave it to you folks he says
and now I'll repossess it

and he carries it away
tucked under an arm like
a baked clay tablet but first
he dusts it off with a hanky

and there's no way of
telling who's going to
hang on and who's not

even on his way back
he may end up spilling some
more of us

THE ROPE

something always holds me back
a word left unsaid
a face suddenly flashing by
a hand clenched into a fist
a daisy
— loves me or loves me not —
and the shame
two little boys
and a woman would
have to live with

but is there anyone who hasn't
felt in his feet
the pleasant tingle
of the final weightlessness

FALL FLOWER

embers with white lashes
ready to flare up
into fire
that's how I stare
into the severe-faced
squinting night:
on every heavenly body
it is you I seek

PROMETHEUS

it's not the chain
nor the clockwork
visits of the eagle's
beak and talons

it's the betrayal's smoke that smarts
the shame of suffocation
why did you people have to set
the woods on fire all around me

THE TREE

an apocalyptic storm
broke over the fields
everyone dropped the hoe
in panic
started to run
with arrows whizzing
from behind
stumbling and slipping
falling flat
glued to the mud
while the sky
fired its cannons

I too was running
but my fear
made me take root
numbed by lightning
to stand still

you on the run
keep on running
flee the storm
do not seek shelter
under my limbs

UNVARIED VARIATION

although the thunders have rolled on
and the lightning bolts have fizzled out
the evening still can make a child of
this old man with autumn hair and gout

standing in the same old hollow tree
where I was at the age of five
when I spent a long night crying
and shouting songs to stay alive

THE DEAD DOLPHIN

head gnawed away
by the carrion eaters of shore and sea
the dolphin hasn't found a way
to bury itself in three days

seagulls are
screeching
above it
around it

conjuring tricks are played
by chaplinesque time
the water makes somersaults
and the chewed head grows back again

sirens
chanteuses
muezzin

the imam calls to prayer

the mace of myths is banging
on the pearly gates of the horizon

waves are tumbling
with thunder on waves
and a human head is

projected by the mind
already on
the frothing wave

the sea goes berserk flooding
our tiny sand castles one by one
the carrion eaters of both the shore
and the deep are watching us

a funeral march groans
its woes under the sea
a cast-off paper crown
is limping perhaps
toward eternity
and the sun
slips
through the muezzin's arms

SENIORS

seated under the barren branches
as if in a staged production or a painting
between each pair of knees a twig
(that will never grow into a rod
it may at most be swished
toward a mangy dog or a
prankster kid with the result that
the dog will growl even meaner
and the kid will pull new tricks
dodging with snickers and making
silly faces — tiny little taps
will quarrel with toothless grunts
and then the sagging trousers will
sink down on the bench to rest
with a twig between the knees
as if they had never moved from the picture)
as if forever and ever

far above the barren branches
a jet plane arches over
the echoing sky and by the time
the faces crunch slowly in its direction
only the long vapor-trail torch
shows where it has fled

it's another flight that's taking off now
under drooping eyelids at speeds faster than light
to someplace where the fall was a donkey
lazily nibbling on hay
and where dawn rose as a gentle butcher
with the screams of chainsaws
and pigs ready for the knife

CONTINUITY

a sacrificial place this was
to pagan gods and then to christ
scattered mossy stones now mark
the shrine where priests once sacrificed

a place where trees and bushes sink
their roots but in the silent loam
your feet detect an ancient path
and always find a god at home

INTO NOAH'S ARK

We must gather, round up everything.
Even words. Not a single word,
nor expression, should be left behind.
Nothing is superfluous.

Let it pour for forty thousand days
and forty thousand nights, if not
one single conscience-stricken bubble
is to ride on the ark's wake.

For at last the water will ebb.
And the mud will dry.

And then from the well-preserved
well-guarded words we'll
re-create the first
wheat kernel of our own,
when we can no longer
live by the word alone.

the pudgy little lad astride the bearded
young man's shoulders sways his gaze from side to side
the two-handled moses-basket forms a bridge rocking
between the father in jeans and wooden clogs with a proud stride
and the pretty little mother in jeans and wooden clogs with brisk
short steps
from them hang bags and sacks bulging with thermos bottles and
cans
of baby food but the two firm wrists hold on to the bridge
where the smaller one's asleep
as safely as within his mother's womb
underneath the asphalt swooshes with all the debris of migrations
and from a pocket of the knapsack gleams
the white passport of happy peace time
a pack of paper diapers

Poems about Poetry
1974-1977

A NOTE ON THE MARGIN WITH A FOOTNOTE

sinuous steps and sinuous gestures
in sinuous interviews
the hallowed happy poets of europe
are jostling for position
in various poses trying
to impress the still impressionable
with their creative quirks
they waddle in twaddle
bumping in to each other

their winged stallions are but
so many barnyard beasts
and for me it's sour grapes

FROM THE UNRECORDED SERVICE REGULATIONS
OF POETRY

on a foray the forward observers
reconnoiter with sharp bayonets stuck on their rifles
with live grenades hung on their belts
and even their tracer bullets are filled with lead

because what matters to the avant-garde is the ammo
    •

(anarchist interjection:)
ban the first person singular
down with words lacking public spirit
    •

pass the drum to the back of the parade
but even there it must be muffled

SHOULD BE ABOLISHED

not only punctuation marks
but capital letters basking
in class distinction
should be abolished
words should be stripped
naked just like
those deported

STILL GOING STRONG

poetry-magistrates
hustle and bustle
make it look like
keeping busy

smoothing things out
doing dance steps
slapping their hands
on their brows

with heads dropped on the table
still bidding the fiddlers
to keep up the fiddle-faddle

graced not with taste
the plastic feathers in their caps
don't do much for them

FROM THE DIARY OF A PILGRIM

I've been stunned by the truly
stunning beauty
of the great cathedrals abroad
but to pray I could be moved
only in my childhood's old
village church
if I could be moved at all

COUNTERPOEM

a variation on Petőfi's "Wolf Song"

please don't let the endless winter
rattle my jaws and jowls
the lone wolf whimpers only and
no longer ever howls

some just froze to death while some
deserted from the pack
and it's in a snow bank where the last
wolf sits and hits the sack

he wouldn't worry if a shotgun
put an end to this
where is now that summertime
freedom-loving bliss

freedom frozen into bones can't foil
lonely hunger pains
you seek a friend whose back to bite but
not one of them remains

All Souls' Day in Vienna
1976

They will braid you too some day
into a wreath with pomp replete
but the world will feel as cold and
strange as this vienna street
you'll go off wheeling like a tram
leaving behind you curled-up tracks

dandelion packs
will swarm the sidewalk cracks

and who'll give you a good goddam

In the whitewashed cathedral of
the augustine order I got to pass
an evening with my back against a pillar
listening to mozart's requiem mass

An orphan even lacks a lone
departed loved one of his own
his tears and wine are vinegar
his candle grows long sooty fur
he's only got himself here and
a single flower in his hand
the truest orphan lacks a lone
departed loved one of his own

The weather was fit for the end of the world
descending in showers the graveyard sky hurled
a flood that engulfed every road in the place
the pallbearers could not see each other's face
waist-deep in water and losing their hold

the unwitnessed tale is still lovingly told
about the crypts dancing like barques loosely bound
and tossing their prancing rumps up and around
the mouse-holes were gurgling like throats with a cough

and that's how the coffin then could've sailed off

on the danube out to sea
and the oceans' waves
on the danube out to sea
and the oceans' waves

floats off a pine coffin
to the oceans' waves
floats off a pine coffin
with music for its sails

Get out of here you pudgy redhead jerk
kicked her heels the bratty chorus girl
and wolfgang amadeus mozart
from the humiliation even redder now
slunk out of the dressing room
the gnädige frau had tired of waiting
the coach was soon to return
the czech doorman was bowing to the cobblestones
as wolfgang amadeus mozart
stumbled out to the street
just in time to catch a glimpse

of the naked stars as they started to bathe
in waves of music surging up there
and wolfgang amadeus mozart
dabbed his damp forehead and chin
and set out on foot for home

on the danube out to sea
and the oceans' waves
floats off a pine coffin
with music for its sails

Is god pleased with praises sung by
men who've had their balls cut off
all neutral voices neutrum
neutrum neutru-u-um

It is said and even recorded in the histoire de la
musique encyclopédie de la pléiade but also
in kolozsvár at number ten vasile alecsandri street
my friend dr. rudi schuller will happily translate
into hungarian german or romanian for those who
don't speak french the part about the grand
travelers les grands voyageurs who claimed
that the inhabitants of the most godforsaken
les plus lointaines civilizations who were totally
indifferent to the tom-toms of neighboring tribes
would perk up their ears only on hearing
mozart's music

Inside whitewashed churches
a prayer very white
my fairy rhyme rings true

inside a blackened church
a prayer very black
my fairy rhyme rings true

inside whitewashed churches
a prayer very black
my fairy rhyme rings true

inside a blackened church
a prayer very white
my fairy rhyme rings true
may the good lord in his
wisdom grant that too

With gaggling geese
quacking ducks
lice-ridden chickens
scab-covered piglets
from a shared little yard
filthy little brats
conceived in boozy haze
in a mob are gaping
at the sky streaked by planes
faster than the speed of sound

stop the world
let it land
let us catch up with it now

In the whitewashed cathedral of
the augustine order I got to pass
an evening with my back against a pillar
listening to mozart's requiem mass

Dies irae dies illa
a wooden hayfork turns a killer
painted eyebrows grace a villa

```
dig   fire   bury
dig   fire   bury
dig   fire   bury
```

should that morning ever break
the sky will be a burning lake
on their feet the trees will bake

fires flamed to be admired
towns in flaming dances mired
hell's chic is now worn and tired

```
dig   fire   bury
dig   fire   bury
dig   fire   bury
```

the judge is the only missing player
as sins inside sins new sins bear
the end alone knows how we'll fare

but our atonement might betray
some ancient sins on judgment day
forcing us again to pay

```
dig   fire   bury
dig   fire   bury
dig   fire   bury
```

and look how doubt makes us mope
for can we truly trust the hope
that none escapes the whipping rope

On june second nineteen-forty-four
the carpet bombing of nagyvárad left a

mother's four fair children under the debris
two four six eight
years old they were when killed
my wife tells the story every year
when she tears that day's leaf off the calendar
this is her poem of peace

who fears hell for this — the one
who lost or the one who won?

sin is the finish and square one

I'm getting used to seeing that
the hand can't stir itself to touch
forgetting its own merry shake and
the gaze had better not see much

the words at first appear so harmless
but then the sentence starts to scratch
hinting at a red alarm with
enough trouble for all to catch

brother come and let's embrace
just once more now let's shake hands
before I fall flat on my face
before you fall flat on your face

My good king my avatar
who was born in kolozsvár
I offer you my candle's flame
it's for you my flower's tame

in hell and heaven a word-feeder
be for us our interceder

My good king my sire
should high heaven's choir
allow you to be heard
please put in a word

for us to have this grand
protocol here banned
things are getting worse
surely for its curse

protect us with your cloak
so fear can't make us choke
on our tongues that we must
bite off in self-disgust

Küküllő-angara
maros-mississippi
küküllő-angara
maros-mississippi

I am headed for home — but he
doesn't believe his own ditty
I am headed for home — but he
doesn't believe his own ditty

crumbling to dust like sifting snow
that's how we live like dusting snow
from szabófalva to san francisco
from szabófalva to san francisco

Lord whoever you are or are not
don't leave us here alone to rot

at your door on tiny wings
a timid prayer scrapes and zings
in a baby's whine but not that dumb
praise be to your kingdom come

What's so wrong with our name
why be shocked so red with shame
have we truly more transgressed
than those hailed as the holiest

maybe we should arm the lungs
with the ancient hebrews' tongues
all we do is mutely nod
daring not dispute with god

beat it bartók beat the drum
your fleeing tails will soon succumb
to the world-wide fire blight
the thatched-roof hut is burning bright

I was thirty-eight years old when
kristina the almost naked fair
maid from styria invited me for a glass
of whisky at the corner of singerstrasse
I'm poor my dear and a foreigner
macht nichts she said it's all souls' day
we finished off two shots each
susanna the pretty german girl whom
you find in tiefengrab's vienna gloom
was für ein gedicht
vier jahrhunderte alt
in her cheeks red roses bloom

forsooth her coral lips can doom
a knight to seek but her perfume

in every lonely tower room
it's in vain though that they seek her
yes I would be your susanna free of charge
but it's a time of mourning all souls' day
there's no need to go into more detail
she gave me a kiss a real smacker
saying it was enough to leave two schillings
on the cloakroom counter

So in the whitewashed cathedral of
the augustine order I got to pass
an evening with my back against a pillar
listening to mozart's requiem mass

Indeed our farm was no big deal
not even god could make us kneel
by hook or crook we managed fine
complaining was not our line
from custom though we used to pray
to keep the old reaper away

Remember me too if you do
the shirt on my back is a soggy mess
like on the fugitive lajos kossuth
when he petitioned the turks
the shirt on my back is a soggy mess
I ad-libbed such a fine speech
with my bad foot firmly planted in the door

so that he could not slam it in my face
for then the long vigil would have been for nothing
the morning star
was still up in the sky
when I parked myself in his doorway
lest I miss him again today
the shirt on my back is a soggy mess
like on poor old lajos kossuth
one hand on the doorlatch and the other
was clutching my stick as tightly as all the swallowed
words were in my throat
I had to be diplomatic
otherwise I was not to achieve my objective
and my small stack of hay might rot
like it did last year that wretched
little hay I cut in the commons
in the commons like earlier as the one-third
that the sexton used to provide
from the village on account of emergency
tolling of the bells that used to go along
with one's share of wheat
the shirt on my back is a soggy mess
while I ask the engineer sir
would he let me have a rig
the harvest is on
all the hands are out in the field
the rig's idle
the horses are fed for nothing in return
it's for the public good that the small

stack of wretched hay should be brought under a roof
only one-third is mine
one-third
we'll see about it by noon or so
hey-you-hey hey-you-hey

he swished the words towards me
by noon or so
how well the stick would have swished in reply
but then there goes the objective and the small stack
of wretched hay hey-you-hey the shirt on my back
was ready to be wrung
like the one on the poor fugitive lajos kossuth

let it burn down where it is
or rot there until judgment day
and now it's not his feet
that bring him but his stick
well over seventy
browbeaten down into the dirt
my dear old dad

Please my lord remember him thus
it was for him you came among us
don't forget him our jesus

let him come to a good end

but ask him about it first before
you have the angels blow the horn

The bright rim of brass petunias
grow fat drops of diamond dew
slapping cherubs on the bun the
conductor gives their downbeat cue

the myth and mass just keep on purling
the soprano leaps from trill to trill

dispensing such unearthly calm
that only eden could instill

the cornmeal's halo steams
the hungry children's dreams

milk murmurs of
milk whirring
milk gurgling
so sweetly
so velvety

what else we need
something to eat
what else we need
to make the blissful
evening complete

the myth and mass just keep on churning
the distant chatter of crockpots
and baked-clay pitchers can be heard

dreams about cud-chewing tender
buffaloes will turn the
poured milk into curd

Tu eşti văpaie fără grai
de dincolo de matca mumii
past the blessed mother's womb
you're the wordless flame who whips
a blaze of itself with the heavenly
wings of an apocalypse

let me have the strength to stay here
and feel my endless blessings fizz
where the night is painted black
by murderous futilities

but neither science nor an eye
can see that a small firefly
transports me to a distant nest
so death and I can say good-bye

They will braid you too some day
in a wreath with pomp replete
but the world will feel as cold and
strange as this vienna street
wie die glocken ihren schall verloren
you will so soon forget your joy

Willy-nilly we must stop
here the sky has turned to tar
something up there casts a dark
shadow on our guiding star

even though there's not one cloud
to the skyless sky now sewn
the rising moon will have to plow
the starless darkness all alone

cliffs and towers will be falling
voiceless in each other's arms
and happiness will smooth out soon
all the wrinkles of the farms

whoever started all this mess
will see it through its final phase
under our careless feet we
feel the ocean's rounded face

Like the bell forgets its ringing
I fast let slip my joy

drop off more wine ye angels on my doorstep
I'm all set to part with this world now
to join those who are free

After all this nothing else can follow
save a levitation as beggarly
as that of a hydrogen atom
but even then I may be pestered by the fear
that they could decide to confiscate
the one electron left to us
        which today
still grants us hope projected
into the next few billion years
and faith in resurrection even
or whatever other myths one hears

Dated 1976 in its final form, Kányádi worked on the poem for over a decade,
adding sections of other texts along the way.

pg. 100 The funeral in the rainstorm describes one version of how Mozart's body was buried and lost in a pauper's grave.

pg. 101 Kolozsvár: the largest city in Transylvania, known in Romanian as Cluj-Napoca.

pg. 101 Vasile Alecsandri: (1818-1890), Romanian politician and writer.

pg. 103 Nagyvárad: Oradea in Romanian.

pg. 104 My good king . . . : Matthias Corvinus of the Hunyadi family, known as Matthias the Just, king of Hungary between 1458 and 1490 during its last flowering before the Turkish invasion.

pg. 105 Küküllő: a river in Transylvania, known as the Tîrnava in Romanian, and a tributary of the Maros (Mureş) River. The Angara is a river in Siberia which Székeler POWs from WWII referred to as the Küküllő, the river of their native region.

pg. 105 Szabófalva: a town in Romanian Moldavia populated by the Csángó Hungarian minority.

pg. 106 The thatched-roof hut is burning bright . . . : This line is taken directly from a folk song.

pg. 106 Susanna the pretty german girl . . . : These lines through the archaic "forsooth" were inspired by the poem *Susanna is a Pretty German Wench* by Bálint Balassi (1554-1594), Hungarian poet and soldier; the 400-year leap backwards is explained by the German text.

pg. 107 Lajos Kossuth: (1802-1894), Hungarian journalist and head of the revolutionary government during the unsuccessful 1848-1849 Revolution and war against Habsburg rule. He died in exile.

pg. 110 Tu eşti văpaie fără grai . . . : these two lines appear in Romanian in the original and are taken from *Logos* by Ioan Alexandru (1941-). The entire poem is translated on the basis of Kányádi's translation into Hungarian in the twelve lines that follow.

pg. 111 Wie die glocken ihren schall verloren . . . : taken from Kányádi's collection of Transylvanian-Saxon folk songs, translated into standard German in the original.

Unadorned Songs
1979-1985

SITUATION SONG

how am I any better
we are civil service
employees all of us

they tell you what
you have to accomplish
they tell me what
I have to write

that pays for the rent
clothing shoes groceries
and if we budget it
for entertainment too

you do moonlighting
for a car and condo
I do it for dewdrops
of immortality
yours is a better bet

THE LUCKY ONE

They see him as the lucky one
my dear old dad now approaching eighty
had his left foot blown off
by a land mine which qualifies him
as a handicapped war veteran for a pension
above and over the social security
as it's told by the other villagers
able-bodied but bent over the years
and not without some envy
yes he had his foot blown off yes he did
but at least he gets paid for it doesn't he
what's true is true and he too
is a war profiteer
just like the major powers
and the arms manufacturers

THE ARTIST

I can't forget the artist whose
easel I helped hold steady
against the playful wind on a late
summer afternoon by a riverside

an idyllic landscape was born on the canvas
with a cow ambling peacefully toward the water

but by the morning I was astonished
to see no trace of the cow and
the earlier vivacious green of the hillside
now singed by the artist
with the rusty brown of drought

where has the cow gone I asked
I had to sell it he said
we had nothing for winter

UNADORNED SONG

I will not speak of
the unspeakable for
fear that it speak its name
crashing down on me
I am no hero
heroes are not
hired help
like us and
the air-traffic controllers
who can be dismissed
with a stroke of the pen
the way lackeys were
with a wave of the hand
in the old days yes
hired help we are
of our own free will for
no one forced us
it's only the force of circumstances
which we all know are immutable
and of course
the hope of a fixed income
and retirement benefits too oh yes
freedom if you please
as a noted critic and prominent
figure remarked
is an eighteenth-century ideal
it is if you think about it
our century dreams of retirement benefits
if we live to see it
that's the way it is isn't it

all around the globe
and perhaps other places too
where civilization
reaches out

Rocket roses are
popped from the cartridge: haiku.
Live ammo for me.

•

Let's have a flower
garden seeded with all words.
Nothing else will bloom.

•

Showers of barbed wire.
Even heaven has lowered
itself to our plane.

•

Pulled in and let out;
the lark is on a leash, I
can tell by its song.

•

Will there be a throat
to shout to the world all the things
we now keep suppressed?

•

Fine, swallow your tongue!
You can get your fill of it
once, but only once.

•

Let the sky be daubed
by old Fra Angelico
and I'll be redeemed.

•

Palm Sunday is here.
we could scrounge up a donkey,
it's Christ's class we lack.

●

Are you held hostage?
At least you know exactly
which side you are on.

●

The no-man's land is
carefully cultivated
while ours lies fallow.

●

Is there a war on?
All our muses are busy
with crossword puzzles.

●

What of country hicks?
Mephisto's a flatfooted
civil service hack.

●

Small nips of the past!
One can get drunk on it but
never quite sated.

●

God, you let it pass,
let the executioners
outlive the poet;

●

they will take you in,
hang you first and then they will
make you resurrect.

●

Why do you remind
me of a clean line from a
Japanese poem?

1.
appellplatz is soaked in silence
and so are the exhibit halls
the tourists are now wintering
where the southern climate calls

someone's punctured one of hitler's
fervid eyes, perhaps a child,
as I leave the guard puts up a
new photo yet undefiled

I sit down for a movie showing
the boredom of the holocaust
as efficient as the looped-
reel film: not a moment lost

Silence. Keeps drizzling. The wind relents.
Appellplatz. Ruhe! A season ends.

2.
you can almost see the same old smoke
rise when a dense black fog attacks
the cleverly constructed
crematory stacks

maybe spring's fresh colors can distract
you from the workshop of the deadly storm
when the poplars guarding the fence
put on their bright new uniform

but now the fog imbues the row
of trees with plaintive danger signs
and the smokestacks with wet snow

where the fledgling flakes appear
to melt as if some dark designs
still kept a fire burning here

3.
in a barrack restored in every
detail (or as a model room?)
I pick out an almost comfy-looking
bunk and could almost assume

possession of it in my mind
as a *für alle falle* ace
a sonnet-sized
sleeping space

where ideas could hibernate
shut off from snow or shine or rain
even if they beat me to a pulp
these ideas might come alive again

beyond all common sense
and serve my heirs as recompense

Space-Crossing Gate
1985-1988

I CONFESS

yes I confess I belong to that small portion
of mankind who without regard to
race religion or even nationality
happen to live or reside
on the top floor

there's no pitter-patter clatter
from anybody overhead
only the rain drums on the roof
taking me back into my childhood
back into our hay-filled hayloft now
tilting empty
                 the sun shines on us with
more heat and the stars are closer to us
our prayers get a head start
over those said below us
                     yes but what if
the building decided to stand on its head
that's what wakes me up at dawn and
as quietly as I can I steal out
into the bathroom and as
gingerly as I can I flush the toilet
I sure don't want to incur the ire
of that old insomniac —
history

TO MY FRIEND KÁROLY KIRÁLY

I too am capable of contemporary heroics
as I walk with you maybe not
all the way to the town square
but along this busy boulevard
a bahnhoffstrasse by european standards
exposing myself to inquisitive eagle eyes
or to the even more predatory
hidden cameras and I
manage to nod or wink at familiar
faces sidling past us
as I keep commanding the whiny fear
inside me to sit and simmer down
but after all it's about
the almost guaranteed future
and present and even past of
two children and a wife
but what a depraved wretch I'd be
if I didn't have the guts
to walk with you at least part of the way
to the town square yes how
laughable even ludicrous my heroic
stroll alongside a fellow human being seems
I remember seeing — I start a story
just to make us look more natural —
I remember seeing the deposed statue
of a hero lying around in the mud of a barnyard

how laughable even ludicrous
was the way the rooster strutted
up and down the statue's corpse
and did his cock-a-doodle-doo
dumping in spurts on the decapitated head

how laughable even ludicrous was the
hero's outstretched arm leading an attack
in the mud of the barnyard but
should they ever spruce up
the broken limbs and
the decapitated head
and put them together on a pedestal
in the proper place
then the hero will be regarded with awe and respect
by all the passers-by

The poem was originally entitled "To My Friend K." to keep the recipient's
identity concealed from the communist authorities. Károly Király was a lead-
ing political figure who courageously represented the Hungarian community
in Romania.

POWER

having spread out our applications
I started to explain my problem
our problem and he just squinted
with narrow eyes and a morsel of a smile
watching the sisyphean struggle
of a tiny little bee caught on the
wrong side of the glass pane and
banging its head against it
only to fall back down as I kept explaining
drenched with humiliation
I felt my shirt and
underwear get soggy wet
at least if the window
could be opened only a crack
so that wretched little bee could succeed
but as if he had read
my thoughts he suddenly
answered: no!

ADJUSTMENT

the eye gets
adjusted to the dark
no use of this dying sun
squinting at me
with head hung low
I trudge on like a one-time
coal-mine horse
put out to pasture

HISTORY LESSON

I tried explaining history
to the stones
they listened quietly

I tried the trees
they kept on nodding

I tried the garden
which gave me a gentle smile

and said that history
consists of four seasons
spring and summer
fall and winter

and now it's time for winter

if our great leader had an inkling
how much electricity buzzes in
my practically paralyzed right
arm and what voltage
throbs in my numb
fingertips in stabs
he would have me
light up this provincial
main street and hook
me up to assembly plants
and perhaps as a generous
reward for my productive
contributions
he would give me leave
on sundays and officially
sanctioned holidays
even during daylight hours
to write some poetry
in his praise

PRIVILEGE

sure we hustle for the privilege especially
at the gala shooting parties
given during the wintertime hunger spells
sure we hustle to be the first
to get our chests slashed open
so that the VIP hunters can
warm up their shivering fingers
dipped into our steaming
innards and boiling blood

SHADOWPLAY

the alarm is raised in the
bureau of shadows
when some man is reported
to be still
unafraid
of his own shadow

the administrators hold a quick
brainstorm and decide unanimously
to withdraw
the suspect's shadow

and after a lapse of time
they issue him
a double shadow

anxiety sprouts in him at once
and slowly mushrooms
into wild terror

they even shadow
my own shadow
mutters the wretched soul
besieged by fear that
even his own shadow
may not be his own

(TRUE) TALE ABOUT THE TYPEWRITER

when the typewriter gets
wind of the fact
that its owner's permit to operate it
has expired
it turns in the keys
the levers get sticky
the ribbon dries out
the carriage gets stuck in the rut

it reacts just like
a law-abiding
self-respecting prostitute
whose health-tag has lapsed
and she stops plying her trade
refusing to expose herself
to the unpleasantness
of possible raids

that's how well it takes to heart
what was drummed into it
over a lifetime

Under the communist regime typewriters had to be registered with the police.

SCREWED-UP RONDEAU

zero zero sixty-five seventy-three
I mumble like a convict who's tattooed
with a number on his arm and memory
the number to my typewriter screwed

this machine providing me with food
is a license-plated yoke to me
illusions don't attack my solitude
zero zero sixty-five seventy-three

my lips are getting black and blued
by hasty words escaping me
even father time has skewed
its human face we used to see
spring's tail is by winter chewed
springs and brooks are ocean's brood
I'd wait but there is none to wait for me
zero zero sixty-five seventy-three

THREE THOUGHTS

Progress

the new roadbed is all prepared
they're already piecing together
the new tracks and the long delayed
streetcar will soon be rolling

but will it ever make a barricade

Precious Stone

toy with words the way
you toy with precious stones
toss them high and catch them again
show one off in your open palm
but do not trade it even for a flute

bare your knuckles for it and grab a throat
but keep it safe between your teeth
and if they throw you to the ground
and pry it loose from you
mourn it till you can weep no more

Trampled Hexameters

we're almost at the point
when even funeral orations
trigger our well-trained
cowardly hands to applaud

SUBJUGATED: FROM THE BOOK OF THE PREACHER

*What has been is what will be, and what
has been done is what will be done.*

what does it mean to be subjugated
asked my younger son at dinner
the food got stuck in my throat
I must have looked startled for the
thirteen-year-old little boy almost
apologetically started to explain
that in the street a lady and a gentlemen
and the latter was cursing which the boy
understood but don't you repeat it
his mother interjected you seem to overhear
everything you're not supposed to
indeed I said but the boy went on
didn't you tell me to ask you everything
I don't understand yes indeed I said
standing up automatically to swing shut
the kitchen window facing the street
and then I fastened it properly
and the look on my wife's face sent me
to the door by the staircase and she even
followed me there to make sure I closed it tight
I get it now you don't have to explain thanks
and the gentleman even howled that
we're about to suffer the fate of the jews thanks
thank you for the nice dinner the boy was sorry for us
he went into the other room while we kept
wordlessly puttering in the third-floor kitchen
whose air had suddenly soured with the windows shut
and from the history of families
living in a ghetto or occupied lands

SPACE-CROSSING GATE

to Tibor Toró

when the news got around in
ever increasing circles
that infinity has no borders
that a world can be imagined
without axioms and postulates
parading as fundamental truths
that through a point several straight lines
can be drawn parallel
to the straight lines drawn around the point
in an imaginary circle
and that circle of imagination
can increase in size to infinite
proportions without borders
they decided for the sake of public safety
to close off infinite space
with a plain pine-beam
crossing gate

AN OLD MAN'S LAST SUPPLICATION

Give me courage to slip
the rope around my neck
and the strength, oh Lord,
to shove off,
                    amen.

MASS-GRAVE SONG

when they started burying
the long vowels executed with
silencer-mounted firearms
it turned out there was a shortage of shovels

a clever subaltern sent for
more infantry spades and the long
minutes of awkward delay
served as an opportunity
for a few of the more literate soldiers
to express their condolences with
mute handshakes eyes downcast

psalms could only be hummed in silence
by the close relatives
of the executed long vowels

god was standing with his back turned

because to him a thousand-year stretch
is no more than the passing of yesterday
or a short night's vigil

FREEDOM OF ASSEMBLY WITH PARENTHESES

they may attend
their theaters (while still open)
   for shows approved by the censors

their churches (while still standing)
   regardless of faith or denomination

their funerals (while still performed)
   till the end of their days in an orderly manner

yes they may attend these institutions
   WITHOUT ANY SPECIAL PERMISSION

BARRACKS BALLAD

a thin little ray of light
once in a while flashes
our eyes begin to see stars
and slowly we're infested
with the tingle of
a hope that perhaps
it's not an illusion to expect
something a little more humane
something with a human face
but then it turns out
that the jailer's little son
was playing with a mirror
a birthday present or perhaps
the guard in the watchtower
out of zealous devotion
or just boredom
started to scan an unscheduled
beam of light
over the carefully
plowed and raked
no-man's land and
that's how our now almost
livable barracks got teased with
the playful little ray of light

BALLAD AD NOTAM VILLON I.

On the crumbling railroad station
splashes a phlegmatic rain,
petty thieves & black marketeers are
counting their ill-gotten gain,
on the front the deaf-mute writing
has its graying hair to show;
huge paintbrushes are in secret
nurturing their beards to grow.

To steal is virtue, and to score
you have to lie, and honesty
is turning dumb without a word,
the power failure is fine with me,
winks the one who asks for light
and gives your chest a playful blow;
huge paintbrushes are in secret
nurturing their beards to grow.

You must be blind if you don't see,
you must be deaf if you don't hear
what's true and what is only said,
the yard-long letters you might smear
will again be sloughed off by
every brick front, high or low;
huge paintbrushes are in secret
nurturing their beards to grow.

Life is typed in lower case,
nothing will forever last,
not even the fright within,
laws and rules in vain are passed,

things can add up in the long run,
some will stand against the flow;
huge paintbrushes are in secret
nurturing their beards to grow.

A pair of glasses would do better,
and no matter what the price,
helping you see things more clearly
than the letters' increased size,
with the losing of your sight
crashes mount up in a row;
huge paintbrushes are in secret
nurturing their beards to grow.

We were thrown in vain as fodder,
the hunger of such multitude
is not so easy to appease
with us as its bone and food,
hate no matter how hard fanned
cannot make the clocks run slow;
huge paintbrushes are in secret
nurturing their beards to grow.

Your highness, glasses don't help him
who's blinded by his haughty glow;
huge paintbrushes are in secret
nurturing their beards to grow.

VAE VICTIS

variations on a theme by the poet A. E. Baconsky

fewer and fewer will listen
even fewer will understand and more
and more Jacob-minded schemers
are peeling poplar bark
while spying on silenced
preachers of futility
born of
              purposely wasted words
that's what his warnings turned out to be as
parables work themselves into raucous laughter
brothers are swinging high sticks
voiceless flutes are hiding out
at the bottom of old haversacks and
triumphant knives are being whetted
to tearfully cut the lamb's throat

MANE AND SKULL
(a fragment)

the third day only finds the mane and skull
the gnawed-on ribcage and spine in disarray
like derailed boxcars piled up in a crash but
nature does its cleanup job without delay

on the third day the reek of rot and wild buzz
of flies surrounds the bloated belly now split
wide open while on the chasm's edge above
the careless droppings too speak of a hasty feast
the silent grass knows nothing of the shame of it
why should this happen to a helpless beast

the third day only finds the mane and skull
the gnawed-on ribcage and spine in disarray
the tired sun trails an empty halter strap and rein
when it skims over the foliage with its final ray

like someone witnessing his own demise
I feel inside me a solemn evening rise
wolves around the scene now gather in a pack
licking their chops as weeping shakes my back

There Are Regions
1980-1992

PROLOGUE

There are regions beauty-laced
lands whose poison's bitter taste
and sweetness on my tongue collide
there are regions deep inside
where the fields give birth to words
and the blooms of mountain peaks
sprout with words embracing them
where my blood flows in the creeks
bounding-babbling through my heart
so in winter I must freeze
to let them under icy armor
twang their little harmonies
spring and summer and fall flash by
as my heirs and ancient kin
there are regions I must wear
on my body like my skin
tortured though they're beauty-laced
lands whose poison's bitter taste
on my tongue can sweetly ride
there are regions deep inside

A PLUNGING WALNUT LEAF

for Sándor Csoori

There are regions where even a summer
dawn can find the water frozen
at the bottom of the well-side trough
its colors hardened
like memory
on top of aging words

with a snort the unsuspecting
young spring colt
backs off
to bolt back to his mother
sniffling scales

squawking about an early fall
and long hard winter
the jays leap far into the sky

down the first
walnut leaf plunges
to land as a wing
on the shoulder
of a man with
frost-infested temples

NATIVE INDIAN SONG

There are regions where
songs do not help bear
daily life's dull load
and the only place you see
some activity
is on the graveyard road

yet the song lives on
protected by a ton
of rubble way down deep
in a guarded nook
of nature's silent book
where it's fast asleep

there are regions where
the common people bear
their silence as a norm
too afraid to talk
they let mute signals squawk
about the coming storm

there are regions where at night
the station has the only light
in waiting rooms as if the smoke
had sparked a flame and from the damp
miasma an after-midnight language
set up a dim nomadic camp
　　in grunts and yowls it flaps around
the horselaugh of the kicked-in gold-capped teeth
it climbs the walls to mount the rafters
throttling the rattle of the railroad fleet
　　shooing away the startled engine whistles
it spreads its flexing muscles to bust a breach
in the ceiling while from beneath your hood
you watch a rite these revelers will reach
in a couple of quick centuries: perched
with dangling feet in an empty windowframe
of saint michael's cathedral these congregants
chalice in hand will toast each other with the same
bold gusto that now makes them bite off the bottle cap
　　my romani brothers let's have another drink
and there goes the alcohol gurgling while
you're still looking for a chance to slink
to a corner with only john's wakeful vision
to guide you plus a baby whose cry starts to race
　　until he's smothered with a gorgeous breast
of life bubblingly bursting in his face
he sucks it as if wine or beer and then the fest
behind your eyelids brings him up gigantic
like the bristled after-midnight language spiced
with its all-devouring big christ

ENGRAVING

There are regions beauty-laced
where the verdure's bitter taste
sours peoples' features and
smothers the last flame of hope
that flickers in their eyes as they
gaze at the frayed end of their rope
a dream can fray and flounder even
as a better end it seeks
mourning kerchiefs and black hats
shadow parched and sallow cheeks
that sit around uneasy like
hands dropped on the bony knees
on rickety benches eaten by
the same dry-rot disease
sit around like in an engraving
down in mexico or far
up north in a vancouver park
where I saw how natives are
apt to sit around and daze
at the last flickerings of hope
hands dropped on their knees they hold
with us the same end of the rope
I was in those distant lands
so sad and shocked to realize
how our own vacant gaze had turned
us into indians with eyes
that a funeral could have hewn
on a sunday afternoon

ARMENIAN TOMBSTONES

There are regions where just ruined churches
and forgotten place names point the way
to armenian helmets or jewish streets
or székeler lands that only yesterday
homed these people but now it's hard to find
anyone who remembers his own kind

there are regions where the grassy mound
alone knows who it is below that chews
the roots because the wooden cross has rotted out
and don't look for the ashes of the jews
or try to read there the armenian text
that the moss-covered marble once possessed

there are regions where the covering slab
with four-leafed clovers in reverse relief
in all four corners for five centuries has
refused to ever crack or cleave
so these old armenian stone crypts
can collect the rain by drops and drips

there are regions where the songbirds migrate
to old cemeteries to slake their thirst
at times of drought from pools collected
in the crevices of tombs where they are nursed
to soar back in the sky and gratefully spread
their song for the souls of the forgotten dead

HE PUNISHES THOSE HE LOVES

like the one jew in the pogrom
of the synagogue
who by chance just happened
to escape the flog

I don't weep with gratitude
dropping on a knee
I don't even try to question
why them and why not me

because so well I know by now
you love me oh my god
when the next time comes around
you won't spare the rod

RONDEAU

Like someone holding in his hand
a rope untied to anything
I look back at the years I've spanned
without a trace now vanishing.

To listen hard I stop to stand
still while bells or leaves may ring
and try to truly understand
the wind that makes my ballad sing

among the branches of the grand
old sycamore where birds can bring
no offspring to the empty and
cold nests held by the age-pruned king
like someone holding in his hand
a rope untied to anything.

Late Poems
1990-2000

BRIEF INVOCATION

Let me lie fallow, oh Lord, for now,
do not put me to work but let
me rest like wheat fields used to
by the farmers' prudent alphabet.

Not only weeds grow there but peace;
it takes a great deal of time to tame
miracles, oh Lord, and it matters
to me how my heirs will speak my name.

More seasons have I marked than lived
like a creek that turns to ice,
picked the strings in winter helping
frozen branches harmonize,
clang to falling autumn leaves,
making each a warning note;
happiness must never be
shoved down anybody's throat.

In drought I hee-hawed for the rain,
so well I played the stubborn mule,
I listened with my feet dug in
to neither wiseman nor a fool,
neither whip nor lashes could have
set me from my course afloat;
not for me the force-fed pulp of
happiness shoved down my throat.

I take a stand as Don Quixote,
a belligerent whiny jerk
wiping shock sparks from my eyes,
not the sunshine's handiwork
but the limelight singed the scream
on the brain of this old goat;
happiness is now again
being shoved down our throat.

Will things, oh Prince, ever change?
How much longer must we bloat
from this pulp of happiness
being shoved down our throat?

UNEXPECTED YELLOW

a note to go under a painting entitled
Unerwartetes Gelb *by András Márkos*

the unexpected yellow
showed up unexpectedly
and yellowed into the mint-
mellow and curdled blood
of unexpectedness
all black lines wiggled into
worms and then a mess of cocoons
so that a capital T fell flat on its back
turning blacker than black when
someone called me a dirty jew
and if I'd walked bent under the weight
of just one millennium before then
unexpectedly I aged by
four thousand years more

THE DOGS OF GROZNY
(a fragment)

the dogs of grozny have all gone deaf and pace
the streets in peace or stand inspecting empty space

above them shriek a thousand rockets and detonator caps
but they just stand there watching silent walls collapse

the clatter of tanks cannot scare them out of the way
they calmly keep on lapping up the bloodpools of the day

when a bullet or shrapnel makes them its mark
they cannot hear the pain no matter how loudly they bark

they found a way to deal
with injustices crying out
to heaven
by slathering the sky
with the plaster
of indifference
and resignation
but first
for safety reasons
they propped it up with boards and studs
at stand-up height

above that
the buzzing rumble
of supersonic carrion-flies
and the screeching of
remote-controlled buzzards
drown out
the plaintive sighs
straying up there

THE WAY . . .

the way you make a visor of your hand
on your forehead stopping every now and then
the way you wander into loneliness
and pass the night not caring where and when

the way you gape at the empty bookshelves
no longer missing the march of books
the way the bed entraps you in the morning
you linger there not caring how it looks

the way your thoughts still stray at times back home
but where's home for you with its welcome mat
the way the word itself becomes outworn
as home frays into just another flat

the way your tongue still treads by habit on
the steps of rhymes like fingers on the keys
the way your face gets coated and it's just
another mirror that your mirror sees

the way the flame gives nothing but its soot
and no one owes a thing to no one else
even sonnets start to paint their faces
from door to door the muse goes ringing bells

the way the glyphs once carved into your brain
now vanish and the unknown is your friend
and secret treasures hidden long inside
are aging with you waiting for the end

the way god claims his place inside you
just as if he were the real thing
like you're the dwelling and its tenant
yes indeed the castle and its king

the way your veins stretch into twanging strings
the soul sneaks out and who knows where it goes
perhaps a volley fired at the sky
will shoo it from here like a bunch of crows

they're laying the pipelines and connecting
even dilapidated old tenements into it
knowing fully well that
it will put yet another yoke of dependency
on their shoulders but
we've shivered too long and we'll know
the price soon enough from the monthly bill
in any case we have no forests left nor force
in our tired backs for the drudgery
maybe the lungs of the earth will keep
us warm for a generation or two before
they collapse with a final gasp and puff
but by then newborn forests will bust out
of the weed-wild fallow fields once
so productive farm lands
and then the rite of saw-borrowing
and the sharpening of the axes will begin
ancient tools will find their way
out of surviving barns and stalls
ancient long-forgotten words will re-surface
from the depths of old cellars
and from the swamp-filled wells of memory
but by then the still vegetating vegetation
might fall prey to desertification
and it will be hard to gather enough firewood
to cook the supper
nothing more than a bundle of twigs and stalks
and perhaps cakes of dried cow dung if cows are still around
or any other droppings dehydrated
by the sun at the time
of world-wide power outages

or else as the old saying goes
those who remain standing at the end
will devour one another raw

Reading the Papers

Associations and clubs,
even academies are formed
and join forces to save
some trees or
flowers or maybe bugs
from extinction;
I'd like to see us Székelers belong
to such a species,
be they trees or flowers
or just bugs.

Four Little Lines of Alarm

The thirst for blood is growing and
so is the need for odes
what is to become of you
oh children of lost roads

a swineherd led into a minefield and horses
scythed down near altars blown to bits
in forests on fire — how come you lord still bother
with this fire-incensed blood-shod rabble who
want nothing but their daily murder fix

your son once already died for them
and now the result is plain to see
their weapon and their shield is hate
why not just get rid of them and create a fresh
new world that's murder- and people-free

your universe is vast enough to spare
a place for all the things that want to live
and worth saving where people cannot tread
I know this kind of talk is quite unchristian
but it's the only sane alternative

let them blow to bits all they have erected
churches bridges labs and homes
and blow away each other as nations and tongues
there isn't a smidgen of compassion or
humility in their boisterous bones

they pray for your help in killing off
each other in murderously pious cants
extend eternal life instead to creatures
whose life is to your greater glory such
as humble animals and plants

AND THEN

The shadows are growing longer and white
like birch trunks and the beginning starts
to curl around to the end just the way
it was written in the ancient charts,

but first the light solidifies in frost-
flowers planted on the windowpane,
and it's no use for a child to try
and breathe a hole in it again and again;

the clockface hangs limp, melted,
and both of its hands have now eloped,
wish wilts over wan reality.
Will it all turn out the way you hoped?

SOMEONE ROAMS ABOVE THE TREES

Someone roams above the trees
turning on and off your star.
Fear haunts all who live unless
dispossessed of hope they are.

Filled with fear and hope I am.
This is my sustaining grace;
fear that leads me by the hand
all along life's twisting race.

Someone roams above the trees.
I wonder when I start my fall
will he light another star
with the sparkles of my call,

or decide to grind me down
to a single dingy corn
forgetting to ignite my soul
on a new star to be born?

Someone roams above the trees who
may know every grain of sand,
may be nothing more than hope,
may hold only fear in hand.

Vivid as it may be, the portrait of Sándor Kányádi that emerges from the poems in this volume will not be complete without a few words about his background and the land he comes from. Standing completely aloof is not a luxury given to the poets of small nations; their fate and their voices are inextricably linked to the very survival of their communities. But this burden of ethnic identity involves not only expectations of leadership, but in creative hands can become an artistic tool and a defensive weapon that in turn serves to define the poet's art and his place in literature.

Central-Eastern Europe has always been somewhat beyond the purview of the English-speaking world, but half a century of isolation behind the iron curtain, followed by a decade of turbulent political and economic change and even scattered ethnic violence, have further muddied the picture. So let us concentrate on the poet's native region, Transylvania, that in a microcosm reflects all the problems of the area, and more.

Transylvania always had a special position within Hungary. For one, most of its Hungarian population belong to a group called Székelers, who were never forced into serfdom. For another, the province managed to retain its independence even during the Turkish occupation in the 16th and 17th centuries, an occupation that devastated most of the country and left the rest in the hands of the Hapsburgs. Thus Transylvania was not only the historic cradle of Hungarian culture but its citadel. WWI changed this. Hungary ended up on the losing side and was severely penalized for it by the Treaty of Versailles: it was chopped up and awarded to the surrounding nations with a small nucleus left in the middle. Transylvania became Romania's booty — undoubtedly a great loss for Hungary, but an even worse fate for the two and a half million Hungarians living there who consequently sank into an inferior, second-class minority status.

The situation was aggravated after WWII by a totalitarian communist regime that sought to establish its own brand of proletarian internationalism through the suppression of minorities, condemning their clinging to their own language and culture as nationalistic deviation. Ceauşescu was especially fond of bolstering his popularity at the expense of minorities, quite literally in the case of the ethnic Germans, whom he sold to West Germany for $1000 a head, thereby obliterating an eight-hundred-year-old community in just a few years. As Hungarians had no similar exchange value, he tried to get rid of them by bulldozing their villages. Since Ceauşescu's demise more subtle forms of persecution on the part of the Romanian government have been instituted. Despite the sorry state of the economy, huge Greek Orthodox cathedrals have been built in the middle of historic Hungarian communities that are roughly two-thirds Protestant and one-third Roman Catholic (Unitarianism, it should be remembered, originated in Transylvania). History books have been rewritten to demonstrate that Hungarians are interlopers, newcomers whose claims of a thousand-year-old history in Transylvania have been concocted by Hungary to justify its irredentist designs on its lost province. Hungarians are denied as a result not only the right to exist but the very fact of their existence. Unfortunately, this policy of slowly eliminating the old Székeler communities is proving effective — emigration is high, especially among the educated classes, which deprives the remaining population of their leaders and spokesmen.

This historical background might help the reader who is unfamiliar with Kányádi's world as these issues are never explicitly addressed in his poetry. Censorship would have made that difficult before 1989 (his readers became adept at reading between the lines) and, too, Kányádi is not one to preach. For him patriotism is not a badge, it is something woven into the fabric of his soul by his life within his beleaguered community. Under the former regime, for example, the Hungarian Ministry of Culture actually offered him a Hungarian passport and an apartment in Budapest, but he turned it down on the grounds that while it was bad enough for doctors and teachers to desert their homeland, for a writer it was unthinkable.

And yet he distrusts patriotic slogans and cheap nostalgia. His attachment to his homeland, rather than reducing him to mere provincialism, compels him to look beyond its borders. He readily identifies with all oppressed peoples, and it is this universality that makes his poetry accessible even without an awareness of the murky details of Transylvanian history. His contribution to the struggle for ethnic survival is his commitment to the preservation of the language and the culture it serves: there is probably no Hungarian community of any size within the Carpathian Basin where he has not toured, reciting in schools and libraries not only his own poetry but all the Hungarian classics, and always from memory. It could even be said the reading public has voted him the greatest living Hungarian poet by purchasing nearly 30,000 copies of his recently issued volume of collected poetry (first published in 1997 and still in print), a phenomenal sales record for a small country.

In addition to his own prodigious talent (he could probably speak in rhyme for a week without missing a beat), Kányádi has had a rich tradition to draw on. Perhaps the central figure in this tradition is Sándor Petőfi, who in his short twenty-six years, which ended tragically in the war of 1849, achieved the unofficial title of national poet of Hungary. His revolutionary use of simple, direct, everyday language in folksong style has endeared him to readers ever since, and his natural, free-flowing way of handling classical Latin forms established him as the standard in poetry. Over the years his style of poetry has continued to inspire Hungarian poets, even when the message changed and more experimental styles were being explored. In Hungarian it is easy to fill the old forms with natural sounding, modern language to express contemporary ideas, because it is a highly inflected language and very loose as far as word order is concerned.

Kányádi is a master of this contemporary formal poetry. He peppers his lines with playful rhymes and alliterations, and uses repeated rhymes in obsessive pursuit of an idea that is to be crystallized in the last stanza. He uses form to serve the content and to enhance the message. Therefore, a translation that ignores form discards the poetry. On the other hand, slavish adherence to the rhyme scheme might also destroy the poetry in English, making it sound more like a doggerel or a jingle. My solution, in most cases, was to thin out the rhyme, and this enabled me to follow the form without letting it divert attention from the content or disrupt the natural flow of the language. This was a particularly acute dilemma with the poems based on Villon, and here I chose meaning over complete faithfulness to the formal experiment.

Kányádi's free verse is not much easier to translate as he often likes to experiment with language that in a way parodies prose, defiantly becoming almost more prosaic than prose. Stray sentences from official documents might mix with personal confession, and unfinished sentences chase each other breathlessly in search of a precise definition that might then slide into an unrelated image from nature, into a metaphor that pulls the whole poem together, while still conveying a sense of urgency. Sometimes the disjointed words are like stones in a concrete slab that one has to dismantle with a jackhammer in order to reconstruct them in English. Word-for-word translation would only result in gibberish, and indeed, I have had to make compromises for the sake of clarity.

About midway through his career Kányádi dropped punctuation and capitalization, which added to the density of his poems and present an additional hurdle for the translator struggling to convey both the intensity and meaning of the already tightly packed lines. The various styles converge in one long poem, "All Souls' Day in Vienna," a masterpiece that combines impressions of his first visit to the West, the drama of Mozart's Requiem, ruminations about the moral complexities of WWII, references to Hungarian history, and flashbacks of village life. Given its scope — a "The Waste Land," if you will, transplanted in time to a different cultural context — it called for a separate page of notes to help the reader with some of the references and place names.

The cycle of poems in the section "There are Regions" illustrate Kányádi's use of ambiguity to dramatize the universality of his message. He seems to be saying with a shrug: Yes, isn't it strange that there are some regions where such and such things can happen. He does not say "there's a country," maybe because Székelers now have no country, they just happen to persist in some areas as aliens in a country that remains alien to them. With the emphatic plural this sense of alienation is extended to many other parts of the world; it's the shared experience of all dispossessed minorities.

The explanatory notes that dot the text are reserved for local allusions. The more common foreign expressions, mythological and Biblical references are likely to be familiar to most readers. Such references come naturally to Kányádi, who on his first day at school in his village was introduced to the art of writing by an old teacher who chalked on the board: "In the beginning was the Word." Biblical figures were so much a part of his daily life when growing up that they seemed to be his own direct ancestors.

It was tempting to cram into this volume all the poems that had already appeared in journals and thus bore the stamp of editorial approval, but instead we decided to balance out the selection with representative pieces from every style and period of the poet's oeuvre. Though some painful omissions had to be made, none of the poems were abridged; those marked as fragments are parts of works-in-progress, and most of these have been published separately, just as they are presented here.

Kányádi's recipe for a good poem is the same as for making an omelet. Make sure you have the basic ingredients, the eggs, some kind of cooking fat and a pinch of salt. You can add anything else you want, but it will be merely irrelevant fluff without the basics. So I always tried to make sure that those basics survived the transplantation process. Another instruction he gave me as his translator was to make his poems "sound good" in English. The only way I could gauge my effectiveness in that respect was to submit my translations to editorial scrutiny at journals all over the English-speaking world. I would like to express my gratitude to all the editors who have read my submissions and especially to the editors of the over forty journals who have accepted my Kányádi translations for publication, and to Howard Sidenberg who worked so hard with me to make this book a reality.

Paul Sohar
January 2002

ABOUT THE AUTHOR

Sándor Kányádi was born in 1929 in the small Transylvanian village of Galambfalva to a family of farmers. Since 1950 he has lived in Kolozsvár (Cluj-Napoca) Romania. A graduate in Hungarian philology from Bólyai University, he has served as editor on a number of Hungarian-language journals and magazines. Since his first book of poetry appeared in 1955 he has published over a dozen collections. Prohibited from publishing in Romania in the 1980s, he had his books published in Hungary. His translation work includes both Saxon folk poetry and Yiddish folk poetry from Transylvania — in bilingual volumes — as well as contemporary Romanian poets and the major German and French poets of the 19th and 20th centuries. He is the recipient of the Poetry Prize of the Romanian Writers' Union and the Kossuth Prize in Hungary, the preeminent literary awards of their respective countries, the Austrian Herder Prize, and the Central European Time Millennium Prize (2000). Kányádi now divides his time between Budapest and his cottage in the Transylvanian countryside.

ABOUT THE TRANSLATOR

Paul Sohar was born in Hungary and came to the United States after the revolution in 1956, earning a B.A. from the University of Illinois. A poet in his own right, his translations of Hungarian poets have appeared in a wide variety of journals and anthologies, including the bilingual volume *Maradok–I Remain* (Pro-Print, 1997).

DANCING EMBERS
Sándor Kányádi

Translated and selected by Paul Sohar from the Hungarian
Valaki jár a fák hegyén (Budapest: Magyar Könyvklub, 1997),
except "Dogs of Grozny," which is translated from a manuscript.
Foreword by Katherine McNamara
Cover portrait by Imre Zsögödi Nagy
Frontispiece by Endre Szász
Set in Janson
Design by Chaim
This is a first edition published in 2002 by TWISTED SPOON PRESS
P.O. Box 21—Preslova 12, 150 21 Prague 5, Czech Republic
info@twistedspoon.com / www.twistedspoon.com

Printed in the Czech Republic

Grateful acknowledgment is made to the editors of the following
publications where earlier versions of some of the poems in this
volume first appeared: *Albatross; Antigonish Review; Archipelago; Chelsea;
Collages & Bricolages; Cyprus Press Review; The Eagle's Flight; Event; Folio;
Frank; Grain; The Higginsville Reader; Home Planet News; Hunger; The
Iconoclast; Illuminations; Ilya's Honey; Left Curve; Lit Rag; Long Shot;
Modern Haiku; Nexus; Offerings; Parnassus; Partisan Review; Peer Poetry
News; Poetry International; Poet's Page; Rattle; Red Wheelbarrow; Seshat;
Shades of December; South Carolina Review; Time for Rhyme; To Topos;
Whiskey Island; Whole Notes; Windsor Review; Zimmerzine;* and
Maradok–I Remain (Miercurea Ciuc: Pro Print, 1997).

Distributed in North America by:
SCB DISTRIBUTORS
15608 South New Century Drive, Gardena CA, 90248
1-800-729-6423 / info@scbdistributors.com / www.scbdistributors.com